Last Thing at Night

Hugh Lavery.

LAST THING AT NIGHT

An encouragement
for each night of the month

MAYHEW-McCRIMMON
Great Wakering, Essex.

This edition published in Great Britain in 1979 by
MAYHEW-McCRIMMON LTD
Great Wakering, Essex, England.

ISBN 0 85597 265 3

First broadcast as Epilogues by

TYNE TEES

a member of the Trident Television Group

Cover design: Nick Snode
Front cover photograph: Tony Barr

Printed by Mayhew-McCrimmon Printers Ltd.

"Come back and keep still and all shall be well with you; in quietness and confidence lies your strength."

Isaiah 30:15

CONTENTS

Introduction

The following pieces were written for television. The audience was a night-audience and tired people are in no mood for pondering great issues. But some do like to end the day or punctuate it with an insight that gives perspective to the daily burden that makes work seem waste or life pointless. These chapters seek to give point and to impart a peace to hearts ragged with the rush of things.

During the day most of us are Martha, busy with too many concerns and carrying too much weight and worry. But Mary has her place. She may well be the patroness of good listeners. Possibly, we all talk too much and hear too little. This book is for those who seek to listen, to learn and to live.

Work

Some of the best stories are the quickest in the telling. There is one in the Gospel that cannot be excelled for brevity and pith. A man anxious about his wealth and security has not enough space for his corn. I'll build bigger barns, he says. How big and how many he doesn't say. Though one wonders whether they will ever be big enough to satisfy him. The picture of the bigger barns arising and the feverish anxiety of the owner is swiftly sketched. Then suddenly God speaks. This night God requires thy soul of thee.

It is a splendid story because it sets the mind ticking. All sorts of reflections arise. Wasn't the man merely being wise? Or was he? What was his real aim? Safety, I tend to think. A security, a wealth so absolute that he would never need worry again. He would have reached the limit beyond anxiety. But did he? Is there a limit of wealth that passes outside the reach of worry? They say a man who makes a million wants to make two.

But the drive to safety, to salvation is a fact, a universal instinct. The problem is the right way. The most worried people are those who are always bothered about precautions. They are the most afraid. Yet fear is what they are seeking to strangle. Is there a solution to this problem of security, of salvation.

Christ often talked of the folly in worrying

about tomorrow. Perhaps his best-known image is that of the birds and the lilies of the field. They were the models, cared-for but not care-worn. The one who creates will provide. But Christ also tells the story of the foolish virgins who were too happy-go-lucky and the story of the man who buried his talent. He was just too cautious altogether. Christ, then, counsels prudent foresight. But he sees worry about tomorrow as a virus that destroys the muscles and tendons of life and one that makes true religion utterly and completely impossible.

How does he reconcile the two? The need for foresight plus ambition. And the danger of that subtle poison of anxiety. It is not simple. But it is central, central to the whole problem of life. If it is not solved real life never comes our way.

By his advice not to worry about tomorrow Christ wasn't advocating a cheerful complacency. All he was saying was that it is utterly pointless getting emotionally involved in tomorrow's problems. It is that emotional entanglement in the unforeseeable that is so sterile, so wasteful and weakening. Tomorrow is not ours. It is God's unique creation. To the man who built the big barns he pointed this out almost brutally. 'This night does God require thy soul of thee'.

Tomorrow isn't ours. What, then is? Today. Now. Now is the acceptable time. We have a great supply of nervous energy for today, for the job in hand. If we use it in remorse about yesterday or fretting about tomorrow we cannot live, enjoy the only point of time that exists — now. We lose contact with reality, with people and lead a vaporous existence in a self-enclosed world. This is not life. It's more a prolonged nightmare.

And if it destroys life it also destroys religion. For religion is essentially outgoing. Out to God and to people. Religion builds not on self but on God. It cries out for Trust. And trust is not easy. It takes courage. In a sense it involves risk. But the risk comes off. Leaving tomorrow to God is a symptom of true religion. Building bigger and better barns, making money we shall never need is lack of trust. It is trying to save our life single-handed. But Christ said emphatically: He who would save his life will lose it. That is, excessive precautions generate fear and destroy life. True life is true religion. Its foundation is Trust. It keeps fear at bay. It is the key to all life, the natural and the religious.

Parent and Child

You may have heard of the little child who was kneeling at its prayers and at the end added a prayer of its own. It was this — O God, make the bad people good and the good people nice.

It is a very revealing prayer. The child knows who are the supposedly good people. But it finds them unattractive. Now why should 'officially' good people, church-goers perhaps, be unattractive, even unpleasant? Christ said there was only one acid test of real goodness, the end-product. By their fruits you shall know them. There is no other test than this — the end-product, kindness, tolerance, a controlled tongue, evenness of temper.

Bad temper is the virus that poisons many a home. A priest in his visiting sees many a family living lives of quiet desperation because of one bad tempered parent. I say parent, because tonight I am thinking of the children, most of them in bed now, some of them possibly anxious and fretful because of a blaze of temper, a row, or a domestic uproar one can only describe as fearful.

Fear is the source of bad temper, some turmoil deep in the heart of father or mother. The child can sense this. And the child differs from us in being helpless, insecure. It seeks that security from father and mother. They stand for stability, for confidence for those strong qualities we call 'adult'. They insure the child against fear. They are the child's foundation, its footing.

A display of bad temper suddenly shatters this firm footing. The child realises that father — or mother — is afraid, is insecure. And this great big world is a fearful place. It is no longer a cosy, snug world, not a place of love and kindness any more. The beginnings of fear are already in the child. And fear drives out love. There is never any peaceful co-existence of the two. Fear will always drive out love.

Fear also drives out God. I wonder how you imagine God. As kind or as frightening? The answer is simple. You imagine God in the same way as you saw your parents as a child. The child takes its picture of God from father and mother. If they are loving then God is love. If they are uneven, unpredictable, bad tempered, then God is likewise, a figure of fear, unapproachable and, in consequence, unapproached.

Parents carry a great responsibility — the life-long happiness of their children is theirs. Their goodness, their godliness, their life is in your hands. Good temper builds. Bad temper destroys. The parent is the image of God for every child. Can we alter the child's prayer just a little and say — O God make the bad people good, and the good people good-tempered. For that's what the frightened child means by 'nice'. Just that. But it means such a lot.

Truthfulness

If I hear a person described as 'utterly Truthful' I am always deeply impressed. Truthfulness, don't you think, is a rare virtue. I wonder why. Possibly because it presupposes so many other qualities; tact, for instance, courage, and maturity, grown-upness.

Children tell lies. Often because they are afraid or because they are unsure of themselves and want to show off. Truthfulness is something that belongs to the adult. A grown-up who habitually tells lies doesn't seem fully grown-up. He seems to lack stature. His character hasn't that firmness, that surefootedness we associate with mature people, true adults, with the people we depend upon.

Telling the truth isn't easy. By no means. We all talk a lot, and speech is a noble instrument. Conversation can be a wonderful power for good, and simple speech can transform unhappy people into happy people. It can bring consolation to people who are sad, uplift to the depressed, new life to the nervous and faint-hearted. All sorts of people with problems hung on Christ's words and found new life in them. They still do.

But Christ told the truth. His words were surprising, hard sometimes, moving, but always true. Sometimes his words caused heckling, protest, violence even and opposition from the highest quarters. But he spoke on. He spoke the Truth. And the opposition grew. It began a conspiracy. Still he spoke and his speaking cost him followers, then friends, then one of his chosen apostles, finally his life. Quite simply he died for the Truth. And the truth prevailed.

Telling the truth doesn't mean being blunt, being offensive. It isn't an endorsement for the 'I say what I mean' type of person who takes delight in hurting people. To keep silence is often a great kindness and often a great sacrifice especially when people we don't like are being discussed. Silence, then, is indeed golden, priceless.

But perhaps the biggest thing of all is telling the truth to ourselves. I think you know what I mean. You must have noticed how easily we can defend our meanest actions not to others but to ourselves. We can excuse our bad temper — 'after all he deserved it'; our dishonesty — 'after all they won't miss the money'; our spite, our slander. That is the most dangerous form of untruth, building a dream-picture of ourselves completely remote from the facts, a false picture, shatteringly untrue.

The remedy is to turn to Christ's words. He doesn't wound, and he doesn't flatter. He just tells the truth. And his strongest words are for the hypocrites, the dream-picture people, people who have a sham facade, chromium on the outside, squalid within. Such people can't improve. That is the curse of untruthfulness. It's a sort of blindness, and the only cure is to turn to Christ whose whole life was truth and whose truth was life.

Innocent Eyes

A very holy man was once asked a question — the sort of question we would all like to put to an exceptionally good person. 'How did you become holy?' And he answered — 'By being very hard on myself and very kind to other people'.

Other people are the one permanent ingredient of our lives. And how we treat them is the master key to whether we are good or bad people. That is the test. That is the answer. Our Lord spent a lot of time talking not about us, but about other people, how to treat them, how to talk to them, and how to see them. Our eyes often see people quite differently from the way they are. Our picture of them is distorted, blurred, prejudiced. The truly accurate picture of other people, clear glass, is rare, very rare.

But the truly accurate picture of ourselves is equally rare. In fact the two go together. The same eyes look at both. And so Our Lord talks a lot about the eyes, meaning these two things, the picture of ourselves and the picture we have of other people. And he assigned a lot of our trouble, our failure to improve to that myopia, that blurred photograph distorting every feature of the other fellow. We have a splendid professional portrait of ourselves beautifully tinted. The other man gets a passport photograph. Christ was a carpenter and he put it differently. He said that we all notice the splinter in the other man's eye, and take no notice of the beam of wood in our own.

The upshot is we can go through life never seeing things as they are, like a man wearing a pair of badly focused sun-glasses. This blurred picture is fatal to improvement, fatal to happiness. We miss the real goodness in other people. We condemn. We dislike. And we are filled with negative, destructive emotions which make us sour and cynical and friendless. It can bring on a tremendous loneliness.

Why should this happen. There is a fierce pull in ourselves towards what is called these days the 'ego' — me. And there is a sort of internal conversation for ever going on inside of us, defending, canonising our actions and always criticising, condemning other people's. This internal chatter is weakening, fearfully negative. And it all stems from that false picture, that blurred vision which sees someone, someone possibly quite near to us, wife or husband, brother or sister, in a disastrously unfavourable light. We see clearly enough the splinter in their eye. But we don't see that our negative, hostile attitude is the result of a blockage in our own. So we distort, we dislike and finally dissolve all our love into bitterness.

Our Lord sums up the position very vividly. 'The eye', he says, 'is the light of the body, so that if the eye is clear the whole of the body will be lit up; if the eye is diseased the whole of the body will be in darkness.' It is as simple as that, difficult perhaps, but how enlightening.

The Saddest Sin

Most of us know the story of Judas, how he betrayed Christ's whereabouts for money. We know the aftermath — his sorrow, his despair, finally suicide by hanging. It is the classic story of the bad man meeting a bad end. Or is it?

Deep in most of us, I think, there is more than a spark of sympathy for Judas. We don't excuse his sin. But we do feel for him in his misery, in the terrible heartache and loneliness, in the sheer dead weight of the sin locked up in him. We have all felt it; sin brings on a kind of weariness, an isolation from everything normal, everything good and decent. If only we could get rid of this one sin. Judas said the same, with the same tired sigh. He went back with the money. They laughed at him. He dragged himself away. Remorse festered inside him and turned to despair. He took a rope and hanged himself.

Well, what was Judas' great sin? Betraying Christ. Not at all. We all do that every day. Peter did the same a few hours after Judas. No, Judas' sin was subtler than that, more subtle and more sad. His sin was not asking for forgiveness. Or rather not asking forgiveness from the only one who can and will forgive. That is what Christ is for. That was his life's work. But a very subtle pride tends to make us shy from God and find forgiveness elsewhere. Judas simply craved forgiveness. He took the money back. They just laughed at him. he went to the wrong place, to the wrong people.

Only God can, only God will forgive sin. That is perhaps the last lesson we learn. A priest meets many people who worry horribly about one sin; they have breakdowns, some take their own lives. Yet forgiveness is theirs for the asking. Doctors have told me of people who sicken and die for one sin they believed unforgivable. The weight of sin lies like a stone where the heart should be and Christ is longing to lift it. The tiny but powerful virus of pride prevents them. I have sinned, I must atone. We will do anything to forgive ourselves, take back the money, take our own life.

All that is unnecessary. All that is completely, disastrously un-Christian. To worry about a sin is a worse fault than the sin itself. Judas' betrayal of Christ was not nearly as great a sin as fretting about it, worrying himself, worrying himself to death. If sin sends us to God, a great saint has said, even sin has its uses. To admit the sin, to seek forgiveness, to start again, clean and resolute, that is the pattern of true Christianity. But only in God is there forgiveness of sin. Go to him, humbly, confidently, often. Go to him always. He will refresh you.

Why Sunday?

One of the strangest of our institutions is the English Sunday. Saturday is different from the ordinary day. But there is something normal about it, with its hustle and bustle, traffic and shopping. But Sunday is so utterly different, almost the freak day of the week.

Well, why this difference? To many people Sunday is a kind of vacuum; or a prolonged full stop. Streets are quiet and empty. Even the air itself seems drugged as though it had taken an overdose of aspirin. Sunday comes to mean inactivity, and inactivity comes to mean boredom.

Can our curious Sunday mean anything else? What of the church-goers? What are they doing? If you're unkind you'll say they are trying to be better than other people. That is harsh, and largely untrue, I'm afraid. Actually, the average church-goer is more conscious of his shortcomings than most others. He is not the type that says 'I never do anybody any harm'. Quite the reverse. You see by going to church he is coming into closer contact with God, and you can't come near to God without becoming conscious, very conscious indeed, of your own sins and shortcomings.

Now this may seem to make church-going a very gloomy sort of business. But it isn't so. It's a good thing, not a bad thing, to meet reality head-on, to square up to certain facts which — let's admit it — tend to be submerged during six days of the week. One of these facts is this — that you and I are created. The self-made man doesn't exist. And the fact of being created, of being God's manufacture — not our own, is one of the outsize facts of existence. It has all sorts of repercussions. It means that in everything that matters I depend. For every heartbeat, for every pulse, for the next hour of life I am completely in the hands of Someone else — in the hands of God.

Christians don't find this a gloomy fact. They find it a fact — reality. A child isn't depressed by the fact that it depends on its parents for everything. It is pleased, boasts about it. It loves the fact. And why? Because that fact is the anchor of its life. It loves to depend. On what? On their love. It belongs to them. There is the heart of its happiness.

Going to church is rather like that, getting into line with truth, speaking to God person to Person, saying 'Our Father' for we are, in fact, children of God. The Catholic doesn't go to Mass with a sense of despondency. He knows he is taking part in something real, in an action which does all he would like to do. It acknowledges his state of dependence on God, thanks God for his existence and asks, with confidence, real confidence for help.

These are fine attitudes, right attitudes, right but difficult attitudes. After the hurly-burly of six days from Monday morning till Saturday night you get twisted out of true. It is hard to untwist oneself. It is impossible. But to Christ it is easy. So it is in Christ we do this. We go to the Father with him, gladly acknowledge our dependence, thank him for our life, ask for help. During the week we may have become outcasts, prodigal, wayward sons. At the altar we return — home again, sons of God.

So Sunday, if you like, is the day when we refocus our vision, become square with the facts again. And the supreme fact — dependence and its offspring of strength and joy. God made Sunday worship a command. He knew the weakness of human nature. He knew that six days would take a heavy toll, would drag from God, would cover up the fine, firm truths of existence. So he gave us Sunday to restore us to truth and reality.

Heavenly

Some time ago I read that Mr. Khruschev in a boisterous mood said that Major Gagarin in his space flight saw no sign of Heaven. So they sent Major Titov for a longer search. And this too proved fruitless. This seems just a crude jibe. Yet it makes Christians uneasy. They feel their teaching is badly conveyed so that to sincere enquirers it must seem remote from the granite facts of this life.

Some of you may think Heaven to be a rather naive, Disney-land embellishment of true Christianity. You may accept that the picture of harps and tinsel is just embroidery designed for less sophisticated people than us. But you may have a genuine difficulty. I have heard people say that if religion concentrates on Heaven it is irrelevant. This world is our headache.

But Heaven actually is grounded in the present, in the here and now. How exactly? In just the same way as the end-product is the key to all the details of manufacture. Men building a house must have the finished plan before they lay the first brick. Now Heaven begins building here. It is in line with our present experience. The most prized things in this life, friendship, company for instance, are the stuff of Heaven. The quiet ache in present friendships is their impermanence. Loved ones die or leave us or grow cold. Heaven without good company would not be Heaven. Indeed anyone who does not like thinking of Heaven does not understand it. We are made to like happiness.

But perhaps the deepest dread of Heaven lies in its apparent stagnation, its idleness. People dread it as they dread retirement. How can there be life without action. There can't be. Heaven is not rest from action. It is rest from strain, from pointless bustle and frustration. In Heaven we shall be fully stretched but not strained. There will be action, but there will be no ache.

Here on earth we are vaguely aware of our capacity for big things, for more than we are achieving. Great resources are untapped. There is a drive to do more, give more. This strong impulse to give, to create is, at root, the urge to love. Love is no soft emotion, no swooning sentiment. It is human action at its finest, at its most disinterested. Nothing lights and lifts the personality like disinterested love. Nothing stretches so fully. You will notice how every song, every poem seeks to capture this experience of heightened reality. But the experience is too large, too unwieldy for words, too subtle for song. Yet the heart knows this is Life, Life in capitals, something heavenly.

You may recall two of the things Christ said about Heaven. The first: 'Eye has not seen, nor ear heard . . . ' in other words it is beyond human expression as love is. The other: 'the kingdom of Heaven is within you', it is within human experience, again as love is. It is best regarded as a state rather than as a place, as Mr. Khruschev thought. Heaven begins here. You lay the bricks in the daily plod of ordinary humdrum life. But what keeps you going in wind and weather, through sadness and sacrifice is the vision of the finished building in which there will be warmth and rest and family. For this building is Home. It is labour now, but a labour of love. For Heaven is ours and builds on human foundations. It could not be otherwise. And Heaven is Home.

To live and work without this steady vision of Heaven is to build without plan and without hope of completion. This is slavery, pointless despair. But if you work to a plan and point how different is the labour, how worthwhile, how sweet the sacrifice. A good life becomes good workmanship. Law and commandment become aids to good solid building, not obstacles. As we grow older the building rises and the vision becomes clearer. The life of any saint is just a drama on this theme. They differ from us mainly in being ten times more active, great givers of themselves. And their only pain was in their weakness to give more, to give all. But they knew that day would come. The kingdom of Heaven was within them.

Heaven is no dreamland vision. It is uniquely relevant to earth. It alone imparts point and purpose to living, alone provides incentive. For Heaven is Home. And earth is homesickness — for Heaven.

Faith on Fire

I wonder if you saw a programme on television which I found very interesting. A group of people gave their reasons for believing this earth of ours was flat. And their arguments were unusually interesting. Possibly because holding that the earth is flat is an unusually interesting belief.

To many people belief in God is rather like belief in a flat earth, interesting but beyond verification. But actually belief in God isn't remotely like belief in a flat earth or a round earth or in any natural science. It is knowledge but more like the knowledge you have of yourself. The question 'Who am I?' or 'What am I really like?' becomes alive in adolescence. Then we know ourselves, we know all the answers. Moreover not only do we understand ourselves thoroughly but nobody understands us. Parents, teachers, friends are all hopelessly at sea. And not only do we know ourselves. We know other people. We see right through them and we don't like what we see.

And not only people. The teenager also knows the world and knows what's wrong with it. He thinks the world a rather squalid mess and blames the obtuseness of those in charge. He knows how to put it right. If only he could have ten minutes with the Prime Minister.

Now this teenage knowledge is a kind of faith, a

faith in ourselves. It may be off-balance. It may be intolerant. But it is real. It matters. It influences the adolescent's way of life, his opinions, his politics. It chooses his friends. It decides the way he thinks, even the way he dresses.

Belief in a flat earth does not have such turbulent consequences. But belief in God does. At this late hour it is good to think of the many people in prison tonight because they believe in God. Men with an opposite belief have put them there. Now that is the sort of faith we are talking about, living faith. Belief in God does not merely mean belief in his existence. If a man told his wife he believed in her completely, and then went on to add that he was merely testifying to the fact of her existence there could be trouble. Things might be thrown, his own existence might be in jeopardy. No, this belief in a person is not an assent to a truth but a total commitment, a way of life involving the whole person, the way he lives and loves, his speech and dress, his manners and morals.

Sometimes a person approaching me about religion begins by saying he believes in a Supreme Being. I know immediately he has no faith. You can't live or die for such a nebulous entity. What he has is an intellectual conviction, a valuable one. But his life is not remotely affected by it. When Christian communities first appeared in towns and villages two thousand years ago pagan observers did not comment on their teaching but on their way of life. 'Look' they said, 'look at how these Christians love each other'. They saw the power of this new faith in the way they lived. This faith had force because it transformed their lives from self-regard into regard for others, the one supremely difficult transformation.

True faith erupts into true love. Mere assent to propositions, to a hundred catechisms and creeds is sterile. St. Paul calls such faith mere sounding brass. St. James goes further. Faith which does not result in a good life, he says, is dead.

We hear sometimes of people who have lost faith. It is my experience that their faith has gone dead. The truths remain intact but they have given up the struggle. For living faith involves struggle. It is virtue. To believe in any person involves submission and submission is no easy exercise. To believe in God involves total submission and a sustained tension. But it is the one tension that is beneficent, expansive, an agent of strength not of weakness. The fine things that remain in our civilisation were created by this fine faith. And only this fine and living faith will restore it. Time, however, is running out.

Admiring

To many people the word 'Worship' has an old-fashioned ring rather like aspidistras. It doesn't seem current, up-to-date. What exactly are people doing when they troop sadly to church? A good question.

Worship is not old-fashioned, but it is old, as old as breathing or being in love. When a man kneels down in church he is not going through a rather awkward gesture. He is first of all acknowledging a fact and dramatising his conviction that there is something or Someone more important than himself. A man does not readily kneel to anyone. Humility is difficult. He is not doing what comes naturally. Rather he is going against the grain of all human pretension and frankly admitting that he is not a self-made man. He is thanking God who is his creator. He is thanking God who is his sustainer. He is being devastatingly factual, down-to-earth. Worship is rooted in fact. And the granite facts are often unflattering, humbling.

The Christian kneels willingly and gladly. To be in tune with reality, to face the facts that we depend on Someone for every heart-beat is wonderfully liberating and to be in the presence of Mystery is not mysterious but illuminating. Even the busiest people with three telephones on their desk have their sudden, unsought moments of mystery when they hear an interior voice asking 'Why?' But number two phone rings and they have no time to answer this question. People in lifeboats testify that a prayer sprung to their lips though they did not believe in prayer. The impulse to worship would seem to be world-wide. But it can be suppressed.

Is the man who kneels afraid? In a sense he is. He doesn't show the symptoms of ordinary fear, a sweating brow, a panting heart. But there is a kind of fear. I know if I look at the night sky when it is a glitter of stars I feel a kind of fear. Perhaps you do. It isn't like the fear when a lorry nearly runs you down. Our English language has a word for this mysterious fear, the word awe. It possesses us in the presence of the unknown or the tremendous. Possesses but does not paralyse. Rather, it seems to uplift, enlarge. The blaze of stars does not frighten the watcher. Nor does the nearness of God frighten the worshipper. The worshipper feels awe not fear. It is a healthy emotion. But does it lead anywhere? It leads to admiration.

Admiration is said to be in short supply nowadays. I don't think that is so. Admiration is native to the human heart. But it is true that admiration is often a misguided missile. It goes to the wrong things, to glossy goods and gadgets, or to the wrong people, people not really worth admiring. Millions, you remember, admired Hitler, and we are still reaping the aftermath of that grotesque idolatry.

Does the worshipper confine his admiration to God. Not at all. He wouldn't be a Christian if he did. He admires people more than most. But the Christian admires in people what is God-like in them, what is good. He will admire fields and flowers just as Christ did. Christ saw them as a tribute to their Maker. Their beauty was a pointer to his. Indeed the whole of creation is a kind of silent chorus of worship, a manifesto not to God's existence but to his character. We divine his beauty from his manufactures, his goodness from good people.

But to see needs eyes, eyes that penetrate beneath the surface, from the surface to the symbol, from the symbol to the reality. In worshipping God we begin with awe. But there is a quick passage to admiration. And this still is not the terminus. Admiration leads to love. That is common experience. That is the experience of worship.

God alone is sheer goodness and so constantly lovable. Most people we meet are not lovable. One must probe beneath the surface to capture the element of goodness. It is there. In every bad man there is a good man trying to get out. The agent of release will be our kindness, our love. But for this one needs to see with the kind eyes of God. For this one needs to love with a finer love. But how will we acquire this finer love? That is the secret of the worshipper.

The Lonely and the Loved

The most common word in the popular songs of every country is the word 'love'. And the reason is that nothing is as important as love. In the words of one song 'it's love that makes the world go round'. To love makes for happiness. Not to love makes for unhappiness. Hatred, envy, malice — these are destructive things. And they don't hurt the person we envy. They hurt ourselves.

Yet we choose to do these things. We choose to forsake love. And life without love is hell. Many people find hell an awkward, even an outmoded piece of Christian furniture. If God is love, they say, then Hell can't exist. But if I hate God and man I choose Hell for myself, here as well as afterwards. So it's no use saying God should not send us to Hell. He does not send us. We are free, each one of us. And God won't take away our freedom. Heaven — or Hell — is up to us. Life is what we make it here and hereafter.

People sometimes talk about Hell as lying in wait for the unwary, as though it were a sort of landmine, a trap, something we fall into. It's nothing of the kind. Hell is something we choose, quite coldly, quite deliberately. Men walk into it, with a firm stride, their eyes open, their minds made up. And it isn't even a new experience. Hell, like Heaven, begins here. It would be absurd if good people were somehow caught in the trap of

Hell. Absurd because unjust. Good people who sin, repent. And that is an act of love. Hell is not for them. They are going, however erratically, to Heaven. They have chosen love.

Love is above all, giving. That's where the popular song misleads us. Being in love is easy, snug and sentimental. But love is different. It is often hard work. Precisely because it involves giving. Self-love, self-regard, selfishness burn away real love. They make for loneliness. We talk of a person being eaten up with self-love. It's a good phrase — eaten up. Because selfishness does tend to devour, to destroy the very muscles of giving and loving. A person who chooses self-indulgence may say 'This is the life.' But he will discover that he should have said 'This is the death.' Because life without real love is death. That is why Hell is sometimes called 'everlasting death'. Life minus love equals death. That is the simplest equation of all.

The thing we most cherish in this life is our freedom. It is a golden gift, one God never tampers with. We are terrifyingly free, free even to turn God down, to choose ourselves as all that matters, to live with no consideration for God or for people. It is a life of self, a life of loneliness and lovelessness. But it is ours, a free, personal choice. And we weren't made for that life. Hence it is unsatisfying, killing, hell. We were made for something different, real love, real life. God doesn't decide for us. Always, the choice is ours, real love or self-love, Heaven or Hell, here and hereafter.

Guilt or Sorrow

Have you noticed how the theme of many plays, especially tragedies, is the appalling theme of guilt. Appalling because it so often leads to disaster. Remember the guilt of Judas after he sold Christ. And Judas is merely the best known of those whose sin has carried them to the very heart of disaster.

But a quiet sense of guilt infects most of us. In itself it is not entirely unhealthy. It is rather like toothache. The pain lets us know something is wrong. We can get it put right. Sin should bring guilt. But it should not end there. If we carry the guilt around like a stone in the heart we shall sicken. We shall die.

Yet a priest meets many people whose lives are a prolonged nightmare because of some past sin which they feel they cannot atone for. Of course, they cannot atone. The truth is, the wonderful, liberating truth is that it is not up to us to atone. Christ has already atoned fully, overwhelmingly. Atonement is not our response. Our response is sorrow.

What is sorrow? How does it differ from, say, worry, guilt? This way. Sorrow is extroverted. It looks outwards and upwards, Christ-wards. It admits the fall. It confesses the sin. It promises amendment. It receives forgiveness from God. And then it rejoices at its completely unmerited, its completely gratuitous forgiveness. For forgiveness is pure bonus. God's love has no strings attached.

What of those unhappy people who carry guilt on their backs and never know joy? Why? The reason often is that they misunderstand the unconditional quality of God's forgiveness. They think in human, almost in commercial terms. Everything must be paid for. Tit for tat. I have offended God. Therefore he will get me. This is spiritual imprisonment. A life sentence. A death sentence. And it stems from this disastrous equation of man with God, the most subtle form of pride there is.

The liberating truth is that I am a sinner. And that God loves sinners. This is a truth that many people never fully accept. There is a quiet assumption that God loves me when I am good and turns away when I am not. This is the source of the guilt that hangs round the neck until we weary of living. In story, in life Christ strove might and main to rub out this disastrous misconception.

Two truths must be seized if we are not to succumb to a sad guilt-ridden existence. First — that I am a sinner. This is often admitted. But the second comes less easily. I am a sinner and God loves sinners. We are tempted to think that God loves us for every other reason but that one. Yet it is true. The people Christ found he could hardly help were those who called themselves righteous. The self-righteous. The people who said 'I keep the law.' Christ had to use shock treatment with them. He called them hypocrites, white sepulchres. He had to bring them to a realisation of their real status — the status of sinners. Otherwise he could not help them.

These people, the righteous, could have done

with a sense of true guilt, a healthy, liberating guilt. The sinners, on the other hand, require a strong sense of forgiveness, of the boundless divine love and mercy if their guilt is not to submerge them in a deep despondency. Judas betrayed Christ and let guilt destroy him. Peter betrayed Christ and let guilt lead him to Christ and to liberation. That is the true Christian response. It leads to life and to love. To religion.

The Rat-Race

Before you go to bed I would like you to consider for a moment the fact of religion. I say fact, because that's what religion is, a fact. Not a theory, not a harmless pastime for do-gooders, and not a pious disguise for people who are, beneath the disguise, chronically selfish.

Religion is the answer to a need. You may not have much religion but you have the need, a need to love and serve some cause bigger than yourself. Only that satisfies. Only that fulfils. Everybody, then, has some sort of religion, some one thing he goes after as the big thing in life, the one thing worth while. With Adolf Hitler it was power. Adolf Eichmann says that with him it was efficiency — dreadful efficiency. With smaller people it is money, reputation, respectability. What is it with you?

This means there is a kind of race going on in every neighbourhood, almost a kind of polite and subdued warfare between people. The Americans call it the Rat-Race, quite a good phrase, as people engaged in it tend to lose the poise, the dignity of adult men and women, and become somewhat animal.

Christ came into a world where this situation was already old. He saw the rat-race and it saddened him. Because he loved these people, every one of them. He wanted to save them from this pointless exhaustion. He wanted to restore their poise and dignity. He wanted them to know and possess the right sort of life. And so it was of life that he constantly talked.

You see he loved these people to distraction. He would gladly die for them. It was for the rat-racers he had come. He came to show them the right way to live. He pointed the way by his talks. And he mapped out the way by his life. He invited us to follow — invited, not compelled. This life fired the imagination. It caught on. It was good news, a complete revelation. It made all men free, all men equal. It made the rat-race seem laborious nonsense. So its leaders killed Christ. But the new life survived even that. It still survives.

For Christ not merely taught the new life and lived it. He also imparted it. People say — it is fine, noble, but is it possible? We need money, promotion, even prestige. Christ agrees. He merely says it is a question of priorities. The key question is — what comes first, what is number one? With the new life it is love — of God and of man. Sheer goodness has priority. What is your number one? A good test is the means you would use to get what you want. Would you cheat or lie? Are you chronically mean about money, unable to give, unable to enjoy what you have. Or is your life mainly strain, tension without that wonderful, interior quiet which is so strengthening to the man who is properly adjusted, to the man of God? These are the vital clues, the questions you must answer.

Christ called his way of life the rule of God, the kingdom of God. Love is central to it. Money and the other things are also there. All Christ said was that you should seek first the kingdom of God. The other things would be provided. So there is really only one basic mistake — putting money first. Then you get caught up in the rat-race. You pant along. And this is not true life.

The true life is a revelation to all who try it. Difficult but possible, strenuous but exhilarating. It satisfies and it endures — always.

Opportunity Knocks

The theme of many novels, plays and films nowadays is the same. Life, they tell us, is a career of disillusionment. In youth men feel ready for greatness and the years ahead lie like a rich field waiting to be worked. A fine harvest seems to be assured.

Act II shows the same people ten or fifteen years later. They have lost the light in their eye. The spring has gone out of their step. They speak of this world not with hostility, but with, what is more desponding, cynicism. They are rich in sour slogans: 'It's everyman for himself.' 'You'll be a long time dead.'

Clearly something has died, something precious. And it is often hard to talk to such a man, to get through to him. Like some slow-footed animal he is covered in thick armour. He can't breathe freely or grow. He can't even communicate. Determined not to get hurt any more he has taken cover from the world.

For he has been hurt. This is the ordinary pattern of existence. Every man, every woman reaches a crisis, a crisis wholly unforeseen, wholly unexpected. It usually takes the form of loss, some great support removed. It may be a great wrong suffered, a slander by one he had supposed his friend. It may be a disabling illness, or a bereavement, or some searing disappointment. In every case, something has died. The pattern of life must change. A prop has been removed.

This crisis comes to all, this dying. But its importance lies not in the crisis — that comes to all — but in the response. All responses can be reduced to two. A man can become bitter and retreat like a hurt animal. Or he can rise to this opportunity, transcend the dying, grow in stature. He can become a man.

This moment of crisis is the moment of religion. Life so far has been too easy, too protected, too self-centred. It is God who removes that prop. Then the old comfy, self-centred world falls apart. This is loss, this is a form of dying. And this is opportunity. Because it is one of those rare moments of knowledge, a flash of insight into reality. A man now knows that he is not the master of his fate, his own creator. This dying was necessary. For now he can be reborn, renewed, re-centred. The process is as old as man. First comes the loss and the almost unbearable pain, the humiliation. Then recognition of its purpose. With recognition comes power, a new power, not his own fitful resolution, but power derived, imparted from above.

This, I think, is the oldest, possibly the only drama, in the world. There are many classic instances of it. Just take one. St. Peter. He was a familiar type, the man who believes he is tough, afraid of nobody. This conviction was the main prop of his existence, his centre of gravity. Just a few hours before Christ died that prop was taken away. It was a teenage servant girl who uncovered his basic weakness. Not once but three times he lied to save his own skin.

For Peter that was the moment, the dying, the

opportunity. He had to choose, either to recognise his weakness and re-centre on God, or to choose egoism and bluff it out. He chose rightly. He had committed a sin he thought he never would commit. He had died a little. How many people commit a sin they believed they were immune to? Everybody, I imagine. It is the greatest crisis of all. It is so often the moment of religion.

For Better for Worse

Have you noticed how people will gather to watch a wedding? Everybody, young and old seem to like a wedding. It appears to be one of the elementary human happinesses to see two people dedicating their lives to each other. It's a great moment, a solemn moment, one of those rare occasions in life which evoke both joy and tears.

And it is a solemn moment if you think what happens. Two young people who have lived protected lives, cared for by parents, looked after, helped, sheltered, now leave this life of protection, leave father and mother. They grow up. Childhood ends abruptly when each says 'I will.' What do they will? They will to leave everyone and live with each other, for each other. It is a solemn moment. It could be a sad moment. But it is, in fact, a time of unspeakable happiness.

What makes it happy as well as solemn is the deep love of the young people. Otherwise it would be a dedication to heroic loneliness. But it is nothing of the kind. Their love is real and strong. Their love is not sterile, not a blind alley. For the first miracle of marriage is the child, a new person, a creation or rather a pro-creation, the father and mother partnering God in that amazing act of producing a new life. Here is marriage at its most glorious. Could love go further, could any union be so powerful, so dynamic, so productive. Here is human nature at its most attractive.

For the child is not helpless, though it can do nothing but utter a cry. It has the support, the glad and unstinting support of its parents' love. So why worry. It was conceived in love. It will be sustained by love, not for weeks or months but for years. Without that support the child could not mature could not be prepared for the world. But with that love it will grow strong, confident, balanced. Nature speaks through the child's helplessness, speaks clear and loud one message; that the love of father and mother must be full, unconditional and, above all, enduring. That is all it demands from its parents, not money or luxury or power. It asks only that they shall love each other, and so they shall love the child.

The boy and girl who go to the altar go gladly. They are giving up a lot, the security of a home, a good measure of liberty, possibly the company of friends. But they go gladly. They say 'I will' with conviction and with joy. For though giving up much they are receiving more. They are receiving each other's love. When each says 'I will' it is said simply. Two words, not I will but, or I will if . . .

No, true love is unqualified, unreserved, unconditional. That is its joy and its strength. Otherwise, that dedication on their wedding day would be a sham, a promise without substance. True love is complete, real, enduring. It gives certainty, sureness to the young couple, now man and wife. It gives life and love to the child.

No wonder people flock to see a wedding. They are witnessing something that calls to the best instincts in mankind. They are catching a glimpse of pure happiness.

One World

People sometimes ask what is the real point of Christianity? What exactly was Christ seeking to give the world?

The answer corresponds to the deepest human need. A need which the genius of man is always trying to fill. The United Nations, the Common Market, Nato, Seato, these are all partial, sometimes pathetic, but always praiseworthy attempts to make one world. There has never been one world. Indeed it is a sad paradox that the deepest need of men eludes them. If only we could be One — think what rich benefits would ensue. How soundly we would sleep at nights once the rumour of war ceased to play its disturbing background music to our lives. Man's oldest, man's sweetest dream would be reality.

So Christ who spoke of the deepest needs of the human heart inevitably spoke of Unity. Yet his surroundings were hardly congenial to such a theme. The Jews were a close-knit people with a strong sense of exclusiveness. The non-Jews, the Gentiles, were complete outsiders. Christ was watering very stony ground. But he went on, speaking kindly of all these outsiders, even of the occupying Romans. Yet he reserved his kindest, gentlest, most winning words for the greatest outsiders of all, those called the Sinners. And he did not merely speak of them. He spoke to them. He went into their houses, had supper with them, made himself One with them.

Yes, One with sinners, gentiles, one with outsiders. Here was a new pattern, a new ideal. It is an impossible ideal? It proved too much for the Jews. it is still proving too much for the world. Each one of us clings to the group. Yet we do thrill to the idea of a wide, world-wide, unity grounded on equality of worth. It has been written into constitutions. Its enunciation sounds nobly from political platforms. We warm to this fine ideal. Yet, mysteriously, we have not realised it.

Why? 'All men are equal but some men are more equal than others.' This witticism is one of the wisest and the most wounding I know. One of the most despairing. It reads like an epitaph on our failure to face the implications of real unity.

On that Thursday night, the night before he died, Christ naturally spoke on this most precious theme. Frankly, he saw unity as beyond unaided human endeavour. Men just haven't the tools for this fine construction, for this One World. The impulse, the power, the dynamic of this splendid creation is love, a rare love which is not native to the human heart. It must be given, imparted from above. God who gives life, gives also this Love. He founds this society which knows no distinction. He answers Man's need. So Christ created the Church, at first a tiny organism, but with the divine nucleus generating the power to grow and embrace the whole divided world of men.

This is the whole point of Christ's singular gifts, of Mass and sacraments, of prayer and endeavour. These mediate that unself-regarding love which is native only to God but conveyed to us as pure gift. Strong endeavour, human effort do not have the priority. They are sterile things unless inspired, vitalised by the divine gift. True unity, then, must come from above. That is the point of the Church.

Indeed the tiny Church grew against all human prediction in a world that was more partitioned and more curtained than our own. It is a success story beyond human assessment. The Church was not merely human. It had come from above and Christ was with it, as close to it as man to wife. Though now the Church is divided let us not think the division is final and fatal. For Christ is with the Church. His power is stronger than men's.

Perhaps the best prayer for Christians is Christ's own prayer on that last Thursday night when he prayed 'that you may be One.' And for those of you who are not Christians may we ask that you regard the Church with all its failings as something unique, something worth examining, something central and no mere triviality. For the world aches for unity, and the Church believes it has the answer to this most crying need of the distracted human heart.

Lent and Liberty

There are some words in the Christian vocabulary that strike a rather bleak and despondent note, words like mortification, penance, self-denial. And, as Lent approaches, they occur more frequently.

I think, in fact I know, they are often misunderstood. Self-denial, for instance. Self-denial for the sake of self-denial is pointless and silly. A person who goes all out for slimming isn't doing it for the pain of slimming. She probably wants to look better, or feel better, or dress better. Slimming is just a means. The pangs of hunger are endured to produce something wholly beneficial, wholly joyful.

Yet, oddly enough, Christians are thought to cultivate the rather bleak exercises of mortification and detachment for their own sakes. Not at all. Detachment is just a means. Its aim is attachment, attachment to something better. Mortification is for vivification. You mortify yourself in order to vivify — to have more, not less, life and well-being. Self-denial is for self-improvement So these exercises have a point outside themselves. If indulged in for their own sakes they would be signs of disease rather than of a healthy Christianity.

Indeed they could lead to pride and a dilution of

true religion. And pride is a dangerous trip-wire in Lent. It is never far from self-denial. You may have met the type. 'I've given up cigarettes for Lent, what are you doing?' 'Putting up with prigs like you' one might like to answer. Our Lord was very wise, very circumspect on this valuable but prickly subject. He was alert to the dangers involved. And he was saddened by its perversion in his own time and among his own beloved people. He saw people who advertised their mortification by neglecting their dress, their appearance and by generally looking rather miserable. To parade self-denial is to poison it.

All this dressing the part, said Our Lord, is disastrous. Mortification must be in secret. A secret between two — God and you. Only then will it be healthy and humble. So look your best, dress your best. And if self-denial is making you sad then there is something wrong. It is missing the point. For the point is life and life means joy not gloom. A saint without joy is no saint.

On the whole Christ seems to have regarded with suspicion any extraordinary or spectacular mortifications. Possibly because he was so interested in ordinary people like us. But he did point out the sanest means of self-denial. He called it 'taking up our Cross daily and following him.' Notice that word 'daily'. It is his pet word. 'Give us our daily bread' 'Sufficient for the day.' The daily Cross is the best meat for penance. For each day, as you and I know, provides its ration of difficulty. Difficult people, difficult jobs, a difficult temptation.

These are the real crosses which we must shoulder if we are to follow Christ. They are built into our life. No need to cast around looking for difficulties. A bitter tongue, a habit of slander, a sinful attachment — any of these may be the daily Cross which we have declined to lift and so stood between us and following Christ. One sinful attachment may be all that stands between a good soul and following Christ. It is in Lent that we are particularly called to take stock, to practise detachment, regain our freedom and follow his footsteps.

In Lent we seek freedom, We seek to sever the cord that binds us. We seek to do this reasonably. First, we must use the ordinary means, the Mass, the sacraments, renewed fervour in prayer. And then we must set about this one sin that holds us fast. We must choose something that will aid detachment, something serious, reasonable and appropriate. We must be serious. We must be serene. And, above all, we must be secretive. Just God and me.

Lent, then, is a strengthening time and a time of release. It has nothing to do with gloom or sadness. It has everything to do with following Christ by picking up that daily Cross with a renewed joy and the hope of liberation.

Illness

Illness is the sort of thing we associate with other people. To us it comes as a surprise, an unpleasant surprise. Even just visiting hospital can be an ordeal; to keep company with sickness can be disturbing.

But the sick are always with us. Hospitals are always full, nurses in demand. When Christ entered a village it was the sick they brought to him. He received them gladly. He visited them. Often he healed them. And when illness strikes it is then we realise how much we owe to those who do not shrink from spending their lives in looking after those who can no longer look after themselves.

Illness means suffering. There is no emotionally satisfying solution to the problem of suffering. We ourselves all cause suffering probably every day. We all endure it. We do not seek suffering. Not even the greatest saint courted suffering. Suffering is just there. What one learns in hospital is the varying responses that suffering can evoke. There is the 'Why should it happen to me?' the most negative, frustrating response of all. It reeks of self-pity. It aggravates illness. It degrades the sufferer. And it hampers those who are trying to heal him.

One night when I was quite ill, the surgeon was chatting to me and he told me that during the war he had had the privilege of visiting the Holy Land. I envied him the privilege of seeing the place where Christ had died. Because the right response to suffering was taught there. On Calvary there were three crosses and there were three responses to suffering. On the left a man who suffered for crimes committed but cursed his suffering, writhed in it, increased it. On the right a man who suffered for crimes he had committed and who accepted his suffering to redeem the pain he had caused others.

In the centre was Christ. He alone of men suffered unjustly for he was sinless. Yet he accepted his suffering, offered it, gladly and freely and completely. It worked wonders. Christ was the model patient. He disclosed the secret so dear to those who are ill at home or in hospital, the secret that sickness is not waste nor punishment, but, above all, opportunity. We are all sinners, and in sickness we have the opportunity to offer something, to give something by way of repentance, and to give completely, cheerfully, without asking the reason, without counting the cost.

Sin and Release

It is sometimes thought that Christians are a rather morbid lot and obsessed by the idea of sin. But sin is not an idea. It is a fact. And to face the facts, to be square with reality is not to be morbid. It is, actually, to become strong.

Sin is so stark a fact that men attempt to elude it by transforming it into something else, something less accusing. So now we hear talk of compulsive behaviour, subconscious motivation, diminished responsibility. These things exist. But they are not what is meant by sin.

No matter what jargon we employ the granite fact remains that I sin, and, what is more, I know I sin. Novels, plays on television all hold a mirror up to sin. Seeing the sin of others seems to diminish our own. But we recognise their sins as what they are, as wilful, and as ugly.

The theme of sin was often on Christ's lips. Why? Because it is the deepest unrest in the human heart. And Christ spoke to the heart, above all to the open and humble heart which knew suffering. From sin comes suffering, anxiety, guilt. From sin comes death. Christ had come to give Life.

'A little water will cleanse us of this deed,' said Lady Macbeth looking at her hands, red with the blood of the murdered Duncan. If only it were so simple. So easily she washed her hands of the blood. But the sin in her heart remained and festered. Finally it killed her.

Christ approached the fact of sin uniquely. He did not try either to minimise it or evade it. On the contrary he urged us to accept the fact of sin and our status as sinners. He urged us to be realists. to look at sin squarely. Yet this is the last thing we do. We admit anything except this — that we are sinners. So we bluff, pretend, prevaricate, evade.

Christ urged accepting the truth. For only the truth liberates, sets us free. It enlarges and uncomplicates the most twisted personality. Refuse to face the truth and life becomes a kind of lived sham. It becomes tense, a prolonged strain, a pitiful drama in self-deception. All this is fearfully destructive. It is not real life. Rather is it a kind of tortured dying.

The trouble is that curious power we have of self-excuse which works away inside us like an industrious mole telling us that 'everybody does it' or that 'I can't help it'. Now this isn't true. The trouble is that deep down we know it isn't true. Hence the lie, the tension, the endless ache. Sin not admitted is the deepest ache of all.

Sin admitted — how different. That is the beginning of victory, the turn of the tide. You remember the story of that great wastrel, the playboy traditionally called The Prodigal Son. He seems to have committed nearly every sin in the book. He reached the cliff-edge that faces the sinner — despair. Then he did one good thing. He turned back. He admitted his sin. He did not excuse or defend or evade it.He admitted it.

Now notice that this admission had a sudden effect. It broke his spiritual paralysis. It gave him power to act and to act decisively. Sin admitted does that. It is a restorative, a tonic. He decided to go back.

He admitted his sin. He went back. Theologians have a long word for that double process — repentance. Now what else could the playboy sinner do? The answer is — nothing. No sinner can. We are not asked to. The rest is up to God. The prodigal went back. He expected harshness. He expected rebuke. He got a divine surprise.

For his father was waiting. Waiting for what? To jeer, to sermonise. Not at all. He was waiting to forgive. He asked for nothing of his lost son. He asked only for him to come back. God does the rest.

Forgiveness is perhaps the greatest humiliation. Many sinners resent it. They say my sin is beyond forgiveness. But no sin is too large. God's love is larger. It is the going back which is hard. But which is so rewarding. It is a kind of resurrection as sin is a kind of dying.

Christians are not obsessed by sin but by forgiveness. They are the realists of this world. For them the truth is everything. God's unconditional forgiveness.

Today

One of the words most commonly used by Our Lord is the simple, lovely word 'Today'. Tomorrow, yesterday do not concern him. And he does not want them to concern us. He does not want us to worry about them. Today's quota of trouble is enough.

But I am sure you know people — or perhaps you are one yourself — who seems to have one foot perched on yesterday, and the other on tomorrow. Their balance is precarious, naturally. And they are usually gloomy people, or, at least, harassed, tremendous worriers. They can't get much done, their nervous energy is so dissipated, a lot of it on yesterday, the rest of it on tomorrow. But one man who did an awful lot in his lifetime said 'Now is the acceptable time'. The time to be seized, to be made use of, to be enjoyed is now.

This may seem obvious and easy. Obvious, possibly; but by no means easy. Not to worry about tomorrow means trusting someone who will. And Christ was most insistent that God would look after tomorrow. You may remember how he drove it home, so simply and so memorably to those humble peasant and fisher folk, many of whom lived at a bare level of subsistence. He looked at the sky and told them how well God cared for the birds. And, he added,

God loves you more. Worry, in other words, is basically a lack of trust; no more. And no less. It is not virtue to worry. Quite the opposite, it is virtue to trust.

Shakespeare called the night 'the death of each day's life'. Each day is a kind of life, a pocket edition of life, with a beginning, a middle and an end. There is a wonderful freshness about the new day. It has life, challenge, opportunity. perhaps opportunity is its finest ingredient.

You may say, 'but my life is so dull'. Every day is the same yesterday, today, tomorrow. Forget about yesterday, forget about tomorrow. They just don't exist. Just take today. Now is the acceptable time. Now is the day of salvation. The day of salvation, the day of opportunity to go back or forward, to improve or degenerate, to live gloriously or slowly die.

God will forgive yesterday. He will look after tomorrow. Some day will not be ours. But today is ours, a rich, golden opportunity which it would be folly to while away in waste and worry. Let today be a day of salvation.

Self-Pity

I suppose most of you read, even if it's only the newspaper. At this very minute tomorrow's papers will be rolling out of the presses, with their headlines and stories. What will their stories be about? Accidents, fires, broken homes, a parade of human distress.

There are people who think that religion, as it were, goes in for suffering and distress, takes a sort of morbid interest in it. They think religion spells gloom. Now anyone who thinks that has misunderstood religion. He has also misunderstood suffering. Suffering isn't a thing to be courted, to be looked for. It comes . . . with the morning paper it is there.

What is important is not how to avoid suffering — you can't. What is important is how you deal with it. And the response to suffering is various. War is an absolute furnace of suffering. It makes one man a V.C., another a deserter. You will have noticed the same with illness. There is a type of patient who becomes a finer person, nobler, kinder, unselfish. A kind of radiance seems to surround the sick bed. You like to visit that patient. The patient is as good as a doctor. Suffering has become happiness.

There is, as you well know, another response, and a destructive one. It is self-pity. Here suffering becomes a morbid thing, a tool of selfishness. The sufferer uses his distress to centre the whole world on himself. Friends, parents, brothers and sisters don't count. Neither does God. It is a kind of applied atheism. In the cold grip of self-pity, suffering is a poison. It kills. What does it kill? It kills pity. It kills love. For love is an outgoing thing, 'seeketh not itself'. And life without love is a caricature of life, almost a prolonged suicide.

Christ holds the key to suffering as he holds the key to right living. He didn't choose suffering as good in itself. No. He came to do his work, to show God to man. Man didn't like it. There was resistance. There was, inevitably, suffering. There was, finally, death. But Christ did not bewail the fact of his suffering. He was aware that suffering was woven into the texture of life. So he accepted suffering. And he used it. How magnificently he used it. In those last, torturing hours, not a word of self-pity, not a word of despondency. He accepted suffering. He used it, he used it for others, redemptively.

In fact his last utterance was a cry of triumph. 'It is achieved, the work is finished'. And the work was, in hard fact, done through suffering. Suffering accepted and used. We, regard the crucifix not as a symbol of horror, or of pain. To us it means victory. To us it means life, not death. A new life was born on that scaffold. Just as we don't look on a war memorial as a symbol of defeat so we don't look on the Cross as something merely pathetic. It is a fine Cross, a Victoria Cross. Suffering hasn't run to waste; it has been harnessed and used and made fruitful. Christ was a soldier doing battle, and finally winning. The crucifix is the emblem of triumph.

You may say this is spectacular suffering. What of the suffering of drudgery and waiting, of monotony, long hours, disappointments, the suffering of mothers, for instance. Christ thought of those. He had a mother. She suffered as a mother suffers, in silence. She says little, but she is there with her son at every crisis from the crib to the Cross, waiting, wondering. She accepts it, fully, silently. It was for her Son, for his work. That was enough. She was pleased to suffer as he did, gladly, redemptively.

When you see the Cross do not see the grim scaffold of suffering. The Cross is not empty since Christ was pinned there. It has become an instrument of life, pointing upwards and outwards to a world beyond suffering and beyond death.

Such Splendid Things

A phrase you may often hear in every day conversation is one that I heard only yesterday, 'It is a miracle I'm still alive'. A miracle. Yet there are a lot of people who find it hard to accept a miracle, even Christ's miracles, even the miracle to which he appealed as the great proof of his mission. His resurrection.

Yet the miracle is not such a stumbling block. Perhaps it is our tired, jaded eyes that look at wonderful things and see nothing wonderful. It is dark now. The sun has set. A ship leaving the Tyne tonight will know precisely the second at which the moon will rise. Tomorrow's dawn is in every calendar and almanac. The sun is never late or early. If the sun rose a good twenty minutes late tomorrow morning and set an hour before tea-time we would be slightly scandalised. We might even call it a miracle. We take regularity for granted. We find no wonder in it.

A poet who was once a tramp and spent many a night in the open, sleeping under the stars rediscovered the sense of wonder he had lost as a boy. And in his poetry he asked a question which you and I might well ask ourselves. 'What is this life, if, full of care, we have no time to stand and stare?' To stand and stare. Or perhaps the key phrase is 'No Time'. No time for true living, no time for God.

Yet creation is the great miracle. This old planet spinning away nowhere in particular, the miracle of dawn and sunset of Spring and Autumn, of field and fruit and flower, of life and death and Resurrection. Have we not time for all this?

Like a good workman God has left his signature. His trademark on all his creation. But it has to be looked for. That is why we have eyes — to stand and stare. It has to be contemplated — that is why we have brains. It is meant to be loved. And by loving creation we come to love God, the creator. If we miss this we are not missing something, we are missing everything. We miss God. We have no time for God.

I cannot end more aptly than by recalling the lines of another poet who was also a tramp, but a tramp, this time in the big, busy city of London. He saw Christ working there, among the bright lights and the twinkling waters of the river. And he wrote that:

> The angels keep their ancient places,
> Turn but a stone and start a wing,
> Tis ye, tis your estranged faces
> That miss the many-splendoured thing.

The many-splendoured thing is God, God seen in his own creation, in streets as well as in fields, in saints and sinners, everywhere. To miss that is to miss so much. Just about everything.

Death's Door

There are some thoughts that come upon us frequently but which we push away as too morbid, too depressing. Such a thought is death. There are reminders of death all around. The long column in the evening paper, death on the roads, flood, fire, accident, the news bulletin. We get used to the fact of death. But we insulate ourselves against its reality. We seldom think — I must die.

Yet death is an ingredient of life, the finale, the end-product. It is more sensible to live with the thought of death than to try and shoo it away, frightened by it. A person who lives in full consciousness of the fact that he must die is not morbid. He is — to use the current word — realistic. For death is real, as real as life. And the thought of death makes life vivid, active and wholesome. It teaches proportion, stops a man or woman getting too attached to things that are not lasting and indispensable. A man who rents a house for a short time will not spend a fortune on it. He will see what is important, put that right, and leave the trimmings. And life, for any man, for any woman, is a short-term lease.

It is a good thing at night to compose oneself to the thought of death. You will be surprised how in a short time death ceases to frighten, how it steadies the mind and clears the vision. And night is a good time to think of death because sleep is a kind of rehearsal of death. We leave things behind. During the day many things get out of proportion, little anxieties take on the size of mountains, a tiny disappointment darkens the whole horizon. The present moment blots out the future. But all this is twisted, out of focus. The thought of death helps to restore proportion, helps, in fact, to let us see things as they really are. The important things become important. The little worries become little again. And death itself will not seem so frightening.

Christ often talked of death, and he talked of it naturally, reassuringly. For death is natural, as natural as life. And Christ talked of death as going home to his Father's house. He came to show us the way, asked us to follow him, in life, in death.

But, perhaps, the thought of death more than anything helps to focus our minds on the importance of goodness. During the day all sorts of other things tend to take priority, money or pleasure or revenge. But in the quiet of the night we can put that right. To a dying man money doesn't seem all that important even though he be a millionaire. When Walter Scott was dying he turned to his son-in-law and said something worth remembering. 'My dear, be a good man, be virtuous, be religious, be a good man. Nothing else will give you any comfort when you come to lie here'. That was the voice of experience. And by thinking of death we partly experience it. We harden the mind. We embrace reality. By thinking of death we understand life. The thought of death gives point and purpose to life. Otherwise we are living in a dream-world. And the dream can become a nightmare. But there is no need for this.

Death is, above all, a fact. If we accept it as a fact, it will become a light. Death will lose its terror. And life will have a deeper, richer meaning.

So Many Laws

There are people who say religion is kept alive by fear. In our grandparents' time that was a common view. Alongside it went the easy notion that religion was outmoded for the obvious reason that science was rapidly removing fear from the earth. But now with the hydrogen bomb and its mushroom cloud as the most spectacular fruit of scientific research that argument has become somewhat muffled.

Religion may make a man afraid. If so his religion is off-balance, a burden and not a support. 'Fear not — it is I', that is the chorus of Christ's teaching. He wasn't teaching a fatuous complacency. In fact there are good healthy fears. Fear of disease makes for prudence and improved medicine. Fear of poverty will make for industry. This type of fear is not nerve-wracking, doesn't tear a man apart. It is a healthy incentive.

Religion should make us have the right sort of fear, or rather the right sort of concern. For instance, a man who is worried about his prestige tears himself to pieces and has no nervous reserves to concern himself with what really matters. The fact, for example, that his children may be strangers to him, or that he has no real, rich friendships in his life, possibly even no real love.

Christ was concerned because he valued human

personality and saw so many destroying themselves, letting a fine personality be tortured and twisted by the wrong sort of fear. The neurotic desire for prestige is almost the epidemic of this modern age. But it is an old disease. In Christ's time the prestige seekers were very religious people, the Pharisees, and their concern for esteem made them turn religion into an elaborate show, a parade of empty observances. This saddened Christ. If religious people lose their way there is double reason for sadness.

Christ was concerned too for another mistake religious people make, another false and destructive fear. This was the fear of the law. As children we find it easy to keep the law. God smiles approval; we bask in good report. Then there comes a time when we find we can't keep the law. What seemed easy now seems impossible. What has happened? Nothing. No one unaided can keep the law. The ten commandments were hard enough. The Sermon on the Mount merely makes them harder. Law itself is not a scrap of help. It merely defines, enumerates our duties, catalogues our sins. As St. Paul says, the law kills. It kills our feeling of power to be good.

Christ came not to give laws. He came to give power to keep the law. In other words he had pity on our inability to keep the law. St. Paul, remember, was a Pharisee, and their law was back-breaking. He groaned under its provisions. And he discovered release, he found power over the law, not in Paul, but in Christ. That was the source of his strength, Christ. The law killed him with its demands. But the Spirit imparted through Christ gave victory.

Fear of the law is just fear of our own weakness.

That can be healthy fear. Healthy if it sends us to the source of power and the unending source of forgiveness. The law then ceases to frighten. But the crisis must come, the day when we recognise we can't keep the law. The law then kills. That killing is necessary, humiliating though it is. For then we learn the shining, the golden truth that the law merely makes us conscious of our sin, but that it is the Spirit, given through Christ, that gives us power, life. To possess this truth is to get rid of a fear that haunts, even paralyses, some good Christians. Let them remember 'Fear not — it is I'.

The Cross is the Crux

Christians make much of Holy Week. The veiled crucifix is a symbol of sorrow as Holy Week recalls the last days of the life of Our Lord. It is a week of high drama. It begins on the Sunday with a great demonstration of popularity for Christ. People sing, carry palm branches, and hail Christ as leader. But by the Friday what a change! The same people are demonstrating again with new leaders. And they are shouting for Christ's death. The man they honoured on Sunday, they dishonoured on the Friday. That day he died.

Yet, strangely, Christians call this Friday Good Friday. What was good about it? How can torture and death be good? There is nothing pretty about a crucifix. And the real crucifixion must have been sheer horror. Yet Christ often foretold his death and quite calmly. He knew it would be hard. He seemed to think it would be necessary. And he never seemed to think it would be useless. His followers were always shocked when he mentioned death. No one likes people who talk about their death. To Christ's followers death was the one topic they dreaded. He had promised so much, a new kingdom in which they would have top places. And what if he died?

But Christ went on to predict his death, but in a curious way. He seemed to be giving it a new slant, a new angle. He didn't speak of death as failure, as the end, as the final tragic curtain. There was no pathos, no self-pity in his words. And he didn't use the standard symbols of death, darkness descending, the cold silence of the grave, final parting. In fact, he chose a most extraordinary example, a startling example. He compared death to a seed — these were country people he was talking to — and he said a seed dies when you put it into the ground. It does, of course, as you gardeners know. If it doesn't it remains as useless as a pebble. But if it dies it erupts into a new life, far bigger, far more fruitful, and, indeed, far more useful than its own tiny existence. It produces the life we all love to see in the fields, the Spring corn, a life that will nourish and sustain and build our lives. And all from a seed that died.

That is how Christ saw his death on Good Friday — just a seed dying. Of course, he never spoke of his death in isolation. He foretold he would rise like the seed with a richer, finer life which, like the corn, would be passed on to others. He even said it would be three days later. And, of course, his followers, hard-headed folk, just didn't believe. Many still don't. The human mind is a curious gadget. It is always trying to reduce God to its own trivial dimensions. It doesn't hesitate to edit even God's words, blue-pencilling here, underlining there, and producing an edition abridged to its own petty understanding, in tune with its own sentiments. St. Paul well said that the Cross was outrageous to some, and a stumbling block to others. But it is otherwise to the Christian.

The Catholic does not regard his crucifix as a symbol of horror. He regards it as Christ did — a symbol of life. The seed must die this Spring if we are to have life this Autumn. Christ's death and Christ's resurrection are just two sides of the same coin. Life through death is the spring, the muscle of Christianity. And so Holy Week is Victory week, its Friday is Good Friday, the Cross is the Victoria Cross, victory not defeat, life not death, not failure but success, the one success that always endures.

Who is Christ?

There is only one key question all must ask. It is this. 'Who is Christ'? It was a question often put to him. 'Who are Thou?' they asked.

Who, then, is Christ? Your answer defines your attitude to many of the deep things of life. There were many answers in Christ's own turbulent days. There are as many answers now. Some say Christ was a great moral ambassador, and feel, with that pompous phrase, they have honoured him. Others say he was a genius, a great religious teacher and bracket him with Buddha and Confucius. Here too they believe they have conferred an accolade.

What did Christ himself claim? His claim was gigantic. Never did he speak like a teacher agog with a new scheme of learning. Nor as a philosopher with a brand new theory of existence. He never expressed opinions, never said 'I do feel that . . . ' or 'It might be a good idea to . . . '. He never convened a committee meeting or put forward resolutions. Christ spoke in imperatives — 'Come follow me' — 'Do this in commemoration of me'. And Christ's imperatives derived from one serene indicative — 'I and the Father are one'. He admitted no human equal, Rabbi, King or Caesar. He claimed identity with God. His work stands or falls by this claim to

Godhead. And this is the Wednesday of Holy Week. Time is running out. For it is the last Wednesday of his life.

Christ had enemies and these enemies had power. They tried to needle him, to trick him in argument, to discredit him as a person, to involve him in conflict with authority. These were people who claimed to be great moral ambassadors and religious teachers and they were bent on Christ's liquidation. This was their week.

But Christ had adherents, simple folk mainly. Simple people are like children in their clear instinct for detecting the genuine, the authentic, the sound metal of truth and goodness. They see through the dazzle of argument and repartee. They see even beyond parable and miracle. They divine the man. This man. So different from their scribes and Pharisees with their complex learning and back-breaking laws. They saw this man had something. He had the truth. And truth speaks with authority.

Take just one of these simple folk. It is Wednesday, a warm spring evening. A wealthy family dines on the terrace. There are guests. And there are spectators. All heads lean in one direction to Christ who is the principal guest. Among the spectators is a woman. Like the women of her time she carries a phial of perfume. It was their treasure, so costly that it was used a drop at a time. This woman is intent, listening. Then so moved she comes forward, breaks the precious phial and uses it all, hundreds of pounds worth, merely to anoint his head.

You know her name — Magdalen. Once she traded in love. Then she met Love itself, Love incarnate and her heart was transformed. She was fired to act with the recklessness, the abandon of genuine love. This love has one function only — to give. It knows no economy or calculus, no less or more. It is spendthrift. Like Raleigh casting his cloak before Elizabeth, it is a gesture of extravagance. Somehow it appeals. It lives.

Note the reaction of the company. The wealthy cried. 'Waste'. The pious suddenly thought of the poor and their needs.

Note the reaction of Christ. He smiled. He approved. Then he defended this wild and wasteful impulse. He saw through the extravagance to the noble motive. He detected the symptoms of a true, uncalculating love.

But he saw more. He saw the woman's gesture as prophetic. She had anointed him. And anointing belonged to priests and kings. And a new priesthood and a finer kingship Christ claimed, and would claim again with his blood. He indicated this too. The anointing, he said, was in preparation for his burial. Strange words on a cool evening at a friend's table. But Christ needed no intuition to know that his death was now certain, indeed imminent. For this was Wednesday. Friday was near.

A simple story. Yet even in this tiny episode Christ asserts his claim not to a system or a philosophy but to an uniqueness of personality. Christianity is no law, no system. It is attachment to a Person, a Person who was man, priest, king and God.

The Story of a simple woman's extravagance will be told always, said Christ. For it was linked with him, and above all with his death. And his death would never die. Not even on Friday.

Dread of the Dark

There is something unsettling about the church on Good Friday. An emptiness, a bareness. The veiled statues, the altar stripped, the tabernacle gaping. All this is strange, disturbing. It is as though a light had been extinguished, as though a death had occurred. We long for the familiar surroundings again.

But it is good that for one day we should undergo this strangeness. A light has been extinguished. A death has occurred. And the strangeness we experience on this afternoon, the unease, the sense of foreboding are not unintended. They seek to take us to another time and to another place, to a hill where a man had died. This man was a light. This man was a guide. He had promised much. He had promised to make life permanent, to make it happy, beyond pain, beyond suffering, even beyond death.

Of course, he had enemies. Good men always have. But his followers were not afraid of them. Their leader, their Christ could work wonders. One word of his could rub them out. They were confident. They were fearless. Then, in the space of a few hours, everything had gone wrong. He, their leader, their Christ, was arrested, tried, flogged, and condemned. And now, now he was dead. And he had not raised a finger to resist. He had not said a word in protest. He had even forgiven those who killed him.

Indeed he had not even blamed them. He had blamed no one. Or he had blamed everyone. For he assigned the cause of his death to a poison active in every man, a poison called sin. It is a strong poison. It kills. Christ allowed it to kill him. For Christ realised that the best sermon on sin was death. This poison could not be overcome by sweet words. Let it do its worst. Let it kill God.

Christ died almost alone. His followers were broken men, trembling in hide-outs, afraid for their lives. Now the power of sin made its full impact. Often they had heard him forgive sin with a sweet phrase. It seemed easy, too easy.

But at three o'clock on that Friday they learnt that sin had power to strike, power to wound, power to kill a man who was God. And for three days that bitter truth burnt inside them. It made life hard, bare, empty, intolerably sad. Could sin do so much, even to their Christ? It could. It did.

Today, each bare, sad church merely dramatises, repeats the sadness those first Christians felt on that Friday and Saturday. We know what Sunday will bring, the final surrender of sin, the humiliation of death. But that was something those frightened men and women did not know. For them, sin had won a total victory. They all had many years to live for they were young. They would preach and teach in strange, faraway places. But the lesson of that tragic week-end had scarred them so deeply that it never left them. 'We preach Christ crucified', they announced. By dying, slowly, horribly, Christ had preached his finest sermon on sin. On that rough, coarse-grained wood he had inscribed a lesson that would outlive time.

So, for a day, we share the emptiness and darkness of those good men and women who thought that sin was easily overcome. It was overcome, but not easily. They learnt the lesson of that Friday. All men would sin. So all would suffer. And so all would die. But now, in the wake of Christ, sin would be forgiven, suffering would be a medicine, death would terminate in life. This Friday, then, is Good Friday. The Cross is the Victoria Cross. And death is but the prelude to life.

Spring-Time

'Men fear death as the child fears the dark'. There is a strange and compelling likeness between death and darkness and we tend to fear both. Night is the day's dying. Hope returns with the daylight.

This is the rhythm of the world — a steady rise and fall. Not a direct line, nor a curve upward or downward. The whole compass of creation, field, flower, animal and man subsists in a regular pattern of undulation. Rise and fall, decay and renovation — this is the cadence of things. Night consumes day. Day evolves from night. In this great alternation the two poles are life and death. At odd moments we inevitably ask which is the dominant. When the motion stops — which will prevail?

No one looking at a dead man will dispute the authority of death. A dead man seems almost an offence against nature. If the man is one we loved death becomes the great criminal and the sovereign power. Gesture, speech, smile, eyes in life so vivid — all so easily stilled. Only death can erase the rich and varied content of human personality.

The death of the innocent is pure heartbreak. They are so rare. What of the death of Christ? That great sculpture, the Pietà of Michelangelo, is, somehow, more than a dead son in the lap of his mother. Never before was there such a son. Nor such a mother. On those sustaining shoulders had pressed the weight of the world's malice. He had found divine support in his heavenly Father. Like us he had found human consolation in his mother. But the weight had pressed too strongly. For this Son had claimed to be Life. And he was dead. He had claimed to be the Light of the world and he had been submerged in darkness.

If Good Friday was anguish, Holy Saturday is despair. It is the day of the pessimist, of the disillusioned. For this man had claimed to be the mediator of immortality. Just forty eight hours before he had, in saying good-bye, imparted the Bread of Life. And just forty eight hours before he had been so alive, so wonderfully alive, so richly communicative in the roles of friend, leader and host. Of all nights with Christ this, surely, was the most memorable. Never had he spoken so divinely. And his theme — Life, the new and unsorrowing Life that was to be theirs. Who could forget that supper?

Yet Saturday and its darkness eclipsed the warmth and light of all that had gone before. Death is so physical and so final, it has the power to congeal the mind and harden the recollection. For Christ had spoken not only of Life. He had spoken also and often of death. He had accepted its role in the rise and fall of creation. He saw death ahead, saw it keenly, but differently. For him it was neither futile nor final. It was not something to be evaded. It had purpose. Dark and malevolent it may be, yet it had something. It had — necessity.

Christ loved the countryside and many a revelation is wrapped in the simplest rural image. His revelation on death, for instance. For him death was not a tomb, not an abyss. What, then, was this strange terror of man's imagining? It was, said Christ, a seed put into the soil. No more — and no less. The seed dies, is buried. But not fruitlessly. Its dying is an agent of fecundity, of re-birth. From its dying a richer and more pervasive life will emerge, corn and bread for man's invigoration. It is a fertile extinction. That is how Christ saw his own death and burial as the passage to newer and enduring Life. That is how he saw the darkness as the parent of Light. This was a key revelation. A little life must die that a larger Life will be born.

Still, death will always stir an ache, and darkness will always impart a tremble. This revelation does not assuage the pain. Rather it explains it. It explains the rhythm of creation, the great alternation of light and dark, the mystery of decay engendering renovation. it discloses that death is a necessary agent in the procreation of the larger life for which the human heart aches in light and shadow.

No night, no day. No darkness, no light. No death, no Resurrection.

Manalive

For Christians Easter is the climax of the year. A holiday and a holy day. To a Christian Easter, if you like, is the clue to whole tangled mass of history. It explains everything that has gone before. And it gives point to everything that comes afterwards. It comes at a wonderful enchanting time, when the land is beginning to stir again, when flower and leaf and bird proclaim the return of life. Is there anything we treasure so much as life? Is there any season we wait for with such impatient joy as Spring?

Easter is Spring enlarged and explained. It is resurrection from death, new life, as Spring is a resurrection from Winter. Good Friday seemed to be all darkness, gloom and failure. Easter explains that it was the overture to new and better life. Man's cruelty to man seemed to reach its peak of extravagance and suffering its peak of uselessness at three o'clock on Good Friday. But here, in the concluding act, Easter proclaims that suffering can be fruitful and that death can be Life. But Easter is so rich in meaning, so filled with joy that one is in danger of becoming merely poetic or sentimental.

But Christianity has nothing to do with sentiment. There are people, of course, who reject Easter and so reject the corner stone of religion.

Sometimes they construct a kind of do-it-yourself Christianity. They take odd phrases from Christ's words in Galilee and produce a kind of sentimental digest of the Christopher Robin type of religion. They omit anything that offends their sensibility. Miracle, judgement, hell, death, and Resurrection — these, they say quite blithely, are irrelevant. But real religion is not like this. Because religion deals with love, and love never is and never was sentiment. Love often, perhaps always means suffering, sacrifice. Christ's love is a long panorama of suffering. It reaches its climax in death. And it reaches its explanation in Resurrection. His death and his Rising are part and parcel of his life — the greater part.

To those who say Christ was a great teacher, a great psychologist, I say 'Read the Gospels'. Christ taught, as any good teacher, not by word only, but by action. What he said is verified by what he did. He said he would suffer. He suffered. He said he would die. And he died. He said he would rise, and he did rise. Easter Sunday is the crucial day of his life. St. Paul puts it most bluntly, uncompromisingly, 'If Christ has not risen, all your faith is a delusion'.

Christ's followers had not expected the Resurrection. For them all was over when the soldier stuck his spear into Christ's side and found him dead. To them resurrection of a dead man was incredible. Only the fact made them believe. Thomas insisted on putting his hand into the gash in Christ's side before he would be convinced. But once they saw it was true, then everything fitted into place. All that baffling talk about eternal life — here was the evidence in Christ's rising, beyond suffering, beyond death.

And that strange talk of destroying the temple and rebuilding it in three days. Christ's death was the death also of the system which resided in the Temple. In its place the new temple of his body, the new system, his Church, the body composed of Christ and his followers. All this and much more is lit up on the morning of that glorious Easter Sunday.

Spring is the hope of the reviving year, and Hope is the finest blossom of the Resurrection. With Christ risen, we his followers have everything to hope for. Nearly every fear that plagues us is, at bottom, the fear of death. But with Easter death too is dead. And life has meaning, purpose, direction. Easter is not only the climax of Redemption. It is the climax of creation, the clue to the riddle of the universe, the guarantee that death will issue in life, that Winter, no matter how hard, how killing, will be but the prelude to the life and loveliness of Spring.

Life Before Death

You may ask — what does Baptism do for me? Where is the change in me? It was late at night to an anxious stranger that Christ had first talked of Baptism. He had talked of its necessity to anyone wanting to enter the new Kingdom. It was necessary, he said, to be baptised by water and the Holy Spirit. A strange answer, here was Christ, undoubtedly the most spiritual man Nicodemus had ever met, stressing the need of something that seemed a mere outward symbol, a ceremonial washing. How come?

Here the word sacrament enters the Christian experience. I wonder if you know exactly what it means. You probably remember how Our Lord had a great regard for everything on earth, for water and wine, bread, oil, fruit field and flower. Above all he had a special regard for people, not rich or poor, good or bad, just for people, for you and me. In fact he became one of us, God hidden in a man, a kind of sacrament if you like. He came to give us new life, his life, and because we are men, body as much as soul he chose to channel this life through ordinary household things which he loved so much, bread and wine, oil and water.

A sacrament both does something and dramatises what it does. If you have seen a child baptised you cannot escape the clear picture of washing. But it is more than a washing from the sin it has inherited. Words are spoken. I baptise you in the name of the Father and of the Son and of the Holy Spirit. Amen! The child is baptised into, naturalised, as it were, into God. St. Paul puts it vividly. He speaks of the child being baptised into Christ's death and rising into the new life of Christ's resurrection. In a fine image, he sees the child, as it were, plunging into the water and dying, then emerging clean and renewed, enriched with a fine life. It is the child's own rising a thing made possible, made real, by Christ's resurrection. This it is that gives it force and reality, that makes it work. Otherwise it would be mere ceremonial. But a sacrament is not just sign and symbol. It does what it seems to do. The child is re-born, renewed. The child rises into a new plane and inherits new resources. Baptised, christened, it too is a son of God, gladly, most lovingly adopted.

People sometimes think that Christ's death and Rising are now just part of history, finished. 'If only we had known him personally', they say. Christ's followers were appalled when he left them. Was this the end? Not at all. They soon discovered the reality of the Holy Spirit, prolonging the presence of Christ, making his work always contemporary, his death and Resurrection always effective. Tomorrow some of you may be taking a child to be baptised. It is a rich experience. To see in it a mere symbol is to miss everything. It is symbol; but it is reality. By water and the Holy Spirit the child is re-made, dies and rises, transcends the march of time, shares in Christ's achievement. Baptism is no idle ceremony. It is not an extra. It is a necessity or else Christ's rising is in vain. The child leaves the font christened, a Christian, naturalised into Christ, one of the family.

But what is this new life. It is actually the life everyone is seeking, some through trials and heartaches, some through a dizzy social whirl, some through money. It is what people call instinctively 'the Life for me'. But it begins at the font. We are free men. We can stifle it. We cannot erase it. Our very restlessness is merely a homesickness for God, for a life both satisfying and substantial. We received its beginning at the font. But have we like the man in the gospel story buried it in a field? Or are we using it to advantage, letting it develop and mature to the fullness every one of us desires?

One and Many

If, in an idle moment, you leaf through a book of quotations, you may find it a desponding experience. Wise men so often are sad men and their comments on the human condition a glitter of cynicisms. Take this one — 'The idea gives birth to the organisation, and the organisation kills the idea'. It lays a wreath on every human enterprise.

Such a comment makes one wonder at Christ's assurance, not in himself, but in the odd bunch of men who were to share his own enterprise. We may be too critical but even Christ seems to have been disconcerted by their obtuseness. Philip seems to have outdone the rest in wrong-headedness, yet an ability to misunderstand belonged to them all. Christ showed no disquiet about the intractable material with which he had chosen to work. Yet how could these men stand up to the force and fanfare of governors? How could they square up to lawyers with knife-edge minds and long experience of the court-room. This prospect disturbed them. It did not disturb Christ. He silenced this particular anxiety by an answer that seems curiously naive. When that crisis came, he assured them, the Holy Spirit would speak through them.

The Holy Spirit? They knew Christ. They

understood the Father. Even Philip. But who was this third force? This Spirit? This was a new mystery. Yet it was this Spirit that seemed to harbour the secret of Christ's confidence in these unperceiving men. He knew their insight was opaque, their resolution brittle, their spirit a fair-weather thing, yet he was unperturbed. Every human spirit was smoking flax and the strongest must borrow fuel from a richer source. This would not be denied to men. It had not been denied to Christ.

Christ acknowledged the Spirit as Light and Guide to him through the maze of human perverseness. His adroitness provoked the charge that he was possessed. In a sense he was. The grosser spirits were daunted by the stronger Spirit in him. This power he named the Holy Spirit. Yet none is Holy but God alone.

This Spirit, then, was of God, and in a slow and cautious revelation he quietly disclosed a divine intimacy. The Spirit in the Trinity has for generations sustained the heart and perplexed the mind of men.

Perhaps the mind's perplexity begins in the classroom — with arithmetic. We are schooled to think of 'one' as pure simplicity — almost as nothing. We forgot that this is a mathematician's device and that in living experience pure oneness is a fantasy. One is an adjective not a noun. One finger, one hand, one man. Who will deny oneness to a man? Yet what complexity, not merely in the body, but in the deeper places. Each man has a mind, he has will, he has feelings, quite different functions but resident in the same deep centre — in the same man. There is unity. But there is a great diversity, and these two do not cancel or collide.

They collaborate. Here experience alone is our teacher and mere theory is a helpless spectator. Reality is too rich for its thin categories and tidy definitions.

A greater richness emerges in a human family for here unity and diversity are amplified. Male and female, youth and age, extravagance and experience — yet one family. In this splendid human nucleus diversity sharpens the unity. We cannot explain but merely acknowledge the fact and realise we already stand on the foothills of mystery. The oneness of arithmetic is a pale, bloodless thing by the side of this blazing reality. For in the family we are aware of a spirit and its symptom is neither difference nor unity. It is both. This is the presiding mystery of the world, for the world itself is one, yet how various, how intricate!

Like a good craftsman God had left an imprint of his manufacture. The world proclaims the wonder of God and discloses his presence breathing in things. But our own spirit is a pale light and we need a strong illumination. We inherit the obtuseness of the disciples. We need new eyes to see with, new hearts to feel with. This is the work of Whitsun for then the Spirit in the Trinity became the Spirit in men both clearing the eyes and kindling the heart. Now they knew the Spirit in person and they recognised him as Love. For Love must keep company, it revels in diversity and yet has an instinct for union that makes it the master spirit animating mankind.

This Spirit was deep in Christ. Though strong, its power was held by the press of this too, too solid flesh. For him Resurrection was release — and return. For us Whitsun was the time when the Spirit in the Trinity became our kin, indwelling but not destroying, burning but not consuming, respecting difference, and yet imparting an impulse to a unity greater than the human heart can conceive.

The Sword of the Spirit

The moon is the new adventure. To set foot there the new experience. It will be like nothing on earth. For the moon-world is dead. And what we cherish most on earth is its life.

A dead planet baffles the imagination. In part we can picture it — a garish parody of the earth, a crude waxwork of creation. What we cannot envisage is the sterility of a whole world without leaf or laughter. On earth, one grey windless afternoon can depress our spirits. But an entire world that never blinks or breathes is too much for human invention.

Yet this busy planet was once quite as still. An age ago it was obstinate clay, hostile to fruit and flower. Life did not stir until spirit first pierced this resisting stuff. Then was the real birth of things and we are heirs to that first impregnation. Everything we prize on earth — the song and sound, the surprise — all are offspring of that prime inspiration.

We often talk of the spirit of the age, the spirit of a place, of a man. But what exactly is this fine force? Spirit is a mischievous word and lightly evades the trim categories of definition. The sharpest epigram cannot impale it. It is as fugitive and as wayward as the wind. And as strong. We know it as we know the wind — by its power. We sense its presence in the turn of a leaf as in the vigour of a storm. On earth we are consoled by its energy and will be oppressed by its absence on the moon. For spirit is the heart-beat of creation.

Spirit is life — that is the key equation. And we are all lovers of life and movement. A dead man offends. A dead planet appals. They are uneasy reminders that the spirit in creation is always at war. It lives in contention. At the heart of things there is the sway of two dissenting forces, created and uncreated, matter and spirit, and the life we know and love is the ground-swell of this profound disturbance. Spirit invades matter. Matter resents and resists its intrusion. In the high moments of contest the world is full of the sounds of complaining. The tree bends and sighs in protest. The sea rises in anger. And the dead mass of creation opposes its inertia to the pretensions of this too possessive spirit.

In man, the most sophisticated piece of creation, the conflict is most palpable. For man is the great amphibian. The lives and letters of spiritual men — those in whom the spirit has reached most deeply — are lit by the fire of this profound opposition, and in every literature their stories are high drama. The human soul, it seems, never tires of the episodes of this raw encounter. Instance the letters of St. Paul. He groans in travail in concert with the rest of creation. His is a great heart. But a divided heart and in him the contest becomes an epic.

The original epic is Christ's. In him the Spirit breathed most generously and in him the urge to outlet was most insistent. It is the property of the Spirit to communicate and it will not renounce its possessiveness. It must influence and inspire as fire must burn and wind must blow. In the Christ who walked in Galilee the world saw the flame at its most ardent but even in him the Spirit was oppressed and Christ voiced the stress and strain within him. The Spirit was willing, potent. But it was fleshed in weakness, and though it burned with a rare quality it was never a steady candle. There was flicker and fall. Finally there was extinction. This is the hard law of creation and the Son of man was subject to its enfeeblement. He died through weakness.

Is the Spirit, then, the world's great loser? Did Calvary write the epitaph on its wild pretensions? Not so. Flesh did achieve a crude supremacy, but this was not the end. The sword of the Spirit flashed like flame in Resurrection and in the refined body of Christ the common flesh of creation signs its surrender. Spirit is the Lord of creation — that is the verdict of Easter. Whitsuntide is the season of its diffusion. The Spirit has possessed one man: through him it will possess all. On Whit Sunday men of common clay like ourselves heard the wind of God blowing with the force of an ultimatum and compelling surrender. This is the climax in the long serial of creation. But it is not the end. For it is the Spirit's vocation to inspire, to possess and transform and it will not rest until the last atom of creation burns with a life as full and as fine as its own.